EXPERIENCE
THOMPSON OKANAGAN

FOREWORD

Welcome to the Thompson Okanagan region.

This area is home to prodigious lands protected by chiseled mountain ranges and plateaus, placid waters, and sensitive eco-systems. The Thompson Okanagan bestows you with year-round outdoor adventures, setting you center stage among profound natural wonders and privy to many opportunities of encountering wildlife in their natural habitat.

Encompassing the dynamic interconnections of nature and well-being, this vast region affords plenty of space to challenge both body and mind through its offering of unparalleled eco-adventure tours, world-class ski resorts and spas, and unrivaled culinary feasts paired with world-acclaimed wines.

Named for its two predominant features—the Thompson River and the Okanagan Lake—this astounding region is made up of 90 communities and hamlets and 28 First Nations groups, each uniquely contributing to its authentic voice. The people of the Thompson Okanagan are proud of their heritage and can't wait to share their stories with you.

Likewise, we are eager to share this publication with you. An all-embracing guide to the region, *Experience Thompson Okanagan* truly celebrates the area's intrinsic beauty and distinctive spirit with stunning photography and memorable stories.

We invite you to enjoy the publication—and to also come experience the region your way, creating memories that will last a lifetime.

Glenn Mandziuk, BA, MEDes., MCIP
President & Chief Executive Officer
Thompson Okanagan Tourism Association

Cathedral Lakes Lodge, page 114

Published by

PANACHE

PANACHE PARTNERS

Panache Partners
Dallas, TX
469.246.6060
www.panache.com

Publishers: Brian G. Carabet and John A. Shand
Regional Publisher: Marc Zurba
Art Director: Emily A. Kattan
Managing Editor: Lindsey Wilson
Editors: Katrina Almendarez, Lori Tate,
Rachel Watkins and Megan Winkler
Director of Book Development: Rosalie Z. Wilson
Administrative Manager: Susan Minner

Printed in Malaysia

Distributed by Independent Publishers Group
800.888.4741

PUBLISHER'S DATA

Experience Thompson Okanagan

Library of Congress Control Number: 2014954279

ISBN 13: 978-0-9886140-8-6
ISBN 10: 0988614081

First Printing 2016

10 9 8 7 6 5 4 3 2 1

First Page Photo: Shuswap Tourism, page 135

INTRODUCTION

Experiences shape our views of the world and broaden our horizons. A day's excursion close to home, an overnight stay in another city, an extended vacation abroad—all have the ability to open our minds and transform our perspectives.

In *Experience Thompson Okanagan*, we track fascinating establishments and people across the region to discover what's unique, revolutionary, innovative, and often life-changing about them. These best of the best entrepreneurs and environmental stewards are what make this beautiful part of the world a true destination not to be missed.

Each type of experience has something different to offer. Taken all together, shopping, dining, lodging, relaxing, and fun compose a full understanding of life in the Thompson Okanagan for locals and visitors. Our carefully curated selection of various experiences is a stunning showcase intended to delight and entertain. Enjoy discovering landmark sights and attractions, appreciate arts and culture, relax in style at hotels and spas, indulge at popular restaurants and lounges, and shop at the finest boutiques and showrooms.

Experience Thompson Okanagan is a breathtaking journey through one of Canada's most beautiful regions, inspiring you to explore the world around you.

Experience life to the fullest.

Experience Thompson Okanagan.

CONTENTS

OKANAGAN

THOMPSON

Sandhill Winery, page 94

Poplar Grove Winery, page 86

Penticton, British Columbia, page 77

Quails' Gate Winery, page 92

OKANAGAN

Van Westen Vineyards, page 124

Monashee Adventure Tours, page 56

ANCIENT HILL ESTATE WINERY

A little off the beaten path, Ancient Hill Estate Winery lies tucked away in the rural Ellison area of North Kelowna. Here small lot wines are produced using centuries-old techniques and modern sensibility. Leaving the hustle and bustle of the big city behind, owners Richard and Jitske Kamphuys decided to emigrate from the Netherlands to British Columbia in the early '90s to get closer to nature. This passion for the natural world is evident when visiting the winery, where panoramic views of the surrounding hills are the perfect accompaniment to a glass of estate wine. When Richard and Jitske were coming up with a winery plan, they wanted to avoid a location that felt commercial, instead opting for a vineyard that pays homage to the early years of Canadian winemaking. Situated on one of the Kelowna area pioneer vineyard sites, the land produced grapes as far back as the 1920s. The cooler climate of the location allows for the growth of unusual grape varieties including Baco Noir, Lemberger, and Zweigelt, which give wine lovers something new to enjoy.

The European-style winery emulates the Old World with its wood and stone construction. Jitske is an accomplished artist in her own right, and her work adorns the walls at the winery, adding a personal touch to the atmosphere. All of the wine sold at the winery is produced on-site under the direction of one of the region's best consultant winemakers, Christine Leroux. Richard and Jitske love to share the methods and craftsmanship of winemaking with visitors; tours of the production area are complimentary. The pair can often be found answering questions and chatting with visitors to the winery. Ancient Hill is also available for hosting wedding ceremonies and various special events.

4918 Anderson Road, Kelowna
250.491.2766 www.ancienthillwinery.com

Photographs: top and facing page by Jean-François Bergeron; bottom courtesy of Ancient Hill

Photographs by Jean-François Bergeron

BAREFOOT BEACH RESORT

Imagine a hotel check-in that involves not ascending an elevator to a narrow hallway of rooms, but navigating winding paths to a private beachside bungalow, or "yurt," without leaving Canada. That's what awaits at Barefoot Beach Resort. Owner and founder Max Picton was inspired by the yurts dotting Oregon coastal campgrounds he saw as a child, and decided to offer Penticton something that can truly be found nowhere else in the vicinity. Domed ceilings topped with a glorious skylight make the round structures large, open and airy, and eco-friendly yet climate-controlled. The yurts dot a landscape of gardens interlaced with numerous campsites, all only steps from the lovely and secluded Skaha Beach. Guests enjoy strolling under a canopy redolent of a more tropical locale to reach the resort's other amenities, namely the Sandy Feet Café, Barefoot Beach House Restaurant, and charming marketplace including Valley Hemp Imports, Covert Farms, Second Scoop Creamery, the Barefoot General Store, and Cheeks Beachwear. You'll find refreshing smoothies on the beach at the Banana Cabana and waterfront gear rentals at the Big Dakez Rental Hut, naturally, making the full-service resort the ideal place to relax on and off the water.

4145 Skaha Lake Road, Penticton
855.302.3224 www.barefootresort.ca

Photographs by Derek Hurst

BLACK MOUNTAIN GOLF CLUB

Black Mountain Golf Club is not your grandfather's stuffy country club. This full par-71 challenging golf course is all about fun, as everyone wears bright uniforms and the music plays loudly—there's live entertainment throughout the summer. Priced well below its competitors, Black Mountain offers great value in championship golf in addition to a well-maintained course with amazing vistas of the surrounding mountains.

The course opened in 2009 and was designed by Wayne Carleton, who spent a considerable amount of time onsite walking the land and identifying the underlying features of the property. Owned by Melcor Developments Ltd., Black Mountain employs a team of professionals who make sure that every aspect of the course runs smoothly. The team's hard work is evident as Black Mountain was a 2010 finalist for the best new course in Canada.

The atmosphere in the clubhouse resembles more of a friendly sports bar than a typical golf club—the grill is open to the public. Its delicious food is best enjoyed on Black Mountain's picturesque patio, so even non-golfers will enjoy themselves.

Though the game of golf is constantly evolving, a good time can always be had at Black Mountain Golf Club.

575 Black Mountain Drive, Kelown
250.765.6890 www.blackmountaingolf.ca

Photographs courtesy of Black Mountain Golf Club

BURROWING OWL
ESTATE WINERY

Working toward balance is a way of life at Burrowing Owl Estate Winery. Here, founder Jim Wyse practices a kind of Hippocratic Oath—"to do no harm"—that underlies the creative viticultural and enological practices of the winery.

Burrowing Owl lies within one of Canada's most unique ecosystems, which includes the northernmost tip of the Sonora Desert. The location, on a southwest-tilting, sandy plateau near the north end of Osoyoos Lake, is one of the most highly rated grape-growing locations in the Okanagan and Similkameen Valleys. In 1993, when Jim began replanting the vineyards, which had been carefully selected for their ability to produce world-class, premium quality grapes, the winery was not part of his long-term vision. When he began seeing wines made with his grapes gain recognition, he fully realized the potential of the location and decided to build Burrowing Owl Estate Winery. Construction was completed just in time for 1998's harvest. The site has since been enhanced with a luxurious guest house and a beautiful fine dining restaurant named The Sonora Room.

Photographs by Gord Wylie, Wylie Photography

The varied and deceptively fragile desert ecosystems within the adjoining vineyards continually challenge the environmentally sensitive team at Burrowing Owl, where alternative pest control systems are the standard. More than 100 bluebird boxes and two bat nurseries invite insect-eating guests to stay awhile and dine in the vineyards. Barriers protect ground nests of meadowlarks during the springtime by preventing farm machinery and vineyard workers from inadvertently destroying them. Snakes are safely relocated, while bears and big-horned sheep are discouraged from sharing the harvest, but never harmed.

Today, with its dramatic vantage point in the middle of the vineyard, Burrowing Owl Estate Winery is a winemaking facility that combines state-of-the-art technologies with proven, classic winemaking traditions. Be sure to bring your binoculars.

500 Burrowing Owl Place, Oliver
877.498.0620 www.bovwine.ca

Photographs by Gord Wylie, Wylie Photography

C.C. JENTSCH CELLARS

Walk through the doors of C.C. Jentsch Cellars' charming tasting room, open daily May through October, and owner Chris Jentsch's passion for farming surrounds you. His winery focuses on transforming the finest, sun-soaked Okanagan grapes, grown throughout more than 63 luscious acres on the Golden Mile Bench, into honestly made, premium wines. The Jentsch family has been farming fruit in the area since 1929. Chris grew cherries for years before planting vinifera grapes and selling to other vintners. In 2013, he took the leap and launched his own winery. Together with the winemaker, Chris produces viognier, gewürztraminer, syrah, a five-varietal Bordeaux-style blend, The Chase, and its sister blend, The Dance, a rosé.

Woven throughout the story of C.C. Jentsch Cellars is not only Chris's enthusiasm for the art of fine wine, but also his love for his wife, Betty. In fact, C.C. represents his middle name, Carl, and her middle name, Coelho, which means "rabbit" in Portuguese. The rabbit shows up on the wine label as well, along with a tiger, which are the couple's zodiac signs. As for The Dance and The Chase, their names are also inspired by the wife he loves, and he jests, "One day I am going to catch her."

4522 Highway 97, Oliver
778.439.2091 www.ccjentschcellars.com

Photographs by Paul Eby

THE COVE LAKESIDE RESORT

Daily indulgences are par for the course at The Cove Lakeside Resort, an exclusive haven nestled along the pristine, western shores of Okanagan Lake. A unique fusion of four-star property and premier culinary destination, the West Kelowna resort lures visitors from near and far to relish in its amenities and epicurean delights.

The captivation of The Cove begins with its lush valley locale and extends to the comfortable luxury that envelops guests as they enter the resort. Warm and inviting suites, each with private furnished balconies, offer breathtaking views of the lake and surrounding mountains. Likewise, the impressive vista extends to the Bonfire Restaurant, where Chef Grant de Montreuil's fresh, classic-rustic menu, featuring many ingredients from the restaurant's own vegetable garden, is always enjoyed with a view from either inside or on the waterfront patio.

No matter the season, the getaway is ideally located within close proximity to a wealth of activities—from water sports in the summer to skiing in the winter, not to mention convenient driving access to some of Canada's leading golf courses. One of West Kelowna's most popular attractions, the Gellatly Nut Farm, boasting 100-year-old trees and heritage buildings, is also right next door, while nearby award-winning Okanagan wineries offer year-round tours and tastings.

Of course, at The Cove, plenty of adventure awaits before even stepping foot off the property. In addition to the delectable dining scene at the Bonfire, a private beach, private marina and moorage, barbecue area and fire pits, tennis courts, 16-seat movie theater, putting green, kid-friendly pools and waterslides, fitness center, and full-service spa, are all available to readily indulge guests at every turn.

4205 Gellatly Road, West Kelowna
877.762.2683 www.covelakeside.com

Photographs courtesy of The Cove Lakeside Resort

GALLAGHER'S CANYON & THE OKANAGAN GOLF CLUB

With sweeping blue skies, rocky bluffs, and tall groves of ponderosa pines that frame the immaculately manicured course, Gallagher's Canyon Golf & Country Club is scenic to say the least. The club claims two remarkable courses in this rugged yet refined setting. The Canyon Course, envisioned by Bill Robinson and Les Furber, is a par-72, 18-hole design framed by soaring mountains and rocky bluffs, with miles of orchards and vineyards colouring the surrounding area. For shorter games, the property has a fabulous nine-hole executive course, The Pinnacle.

The GBC Golf Academy at Gallagher's Canyon, featuring a double-ended 300-yard driving range with target greens, bunkers, and chipping and putting areas, is known as one of the finest learning and practice facilities in the province. To refuel after a day on the links, the clubhouse's culinary team will tee up a memorable dining experience using fresh local fruits and vegetables and award-winning wines from the Okanagan Valley.

4320 Gallagher's Drive West, Kelowna
250.861.4240 www.golfbc.com

Bears and quails may seem like an unlikely pairing—unless it's The Bear and The Quail, the two exhilarating courses at The Okanagan Golf Club.

The Bear, planned by Nicklaus Design, is a par-72, 18-hole masterpiece with dramatic sculpted greens, as well as neighbouring forests and sage brush hills, earning it status as the crown jewel of the valley. The Bear is a marvel of both manmade design and natural harmony with its well-placed bunkers, generous fairways, tiered greens, and scenic views of Lake McIvor. The 6,885-yard course opened in 1999, and its signature 3rd hole has been testing ambitious players ever since.

The Quail, designed by Les Furber and built in 1994, features multi-tiered fairways and remarkable elevation changes for an exhilarating game. Its nearly 6,800 yards of fairways meander around a majestic rock bluff. Breathtaking vistas and natural splendor surround every hole, especially the signature 18th. Together The Bear and The Quail form an irresistible combination, making The Okanagan Golf Club a true destination for connoisseurs of the great game.

3200 Via Centrale, Kelowna
250.765.5955 www.golfbc.com

Photographs by The Henebrys

HILLSIDE WINERY & BISTRO

Land that was once home to early 20th-century apricot groves now produces fruit for a different purpose at Hillside Winery & Bistro. Originally an orchard owned by the Riddle family, the gravelly soil now reveals more than 20 acres of terraced grapevines that create some of the region's most sought-after wines: cabernet Franc, syrah, gewürztraminer, and the trademark blend Mosaic. The winery began to take shape after being purchased by two Czechoslovakian immigrants in 1979, with the first grape plantings five years later. Under ideal Okanagan weather conditions, the vines thrived and a longtime business was born. One lone apricot tree remains on the property's Kettle Valley Railway today, serving as a reminder of the winery's beginnings and history in the community.

Photographs by Chris Cornett

Focused on growing the best grapes with the least amount of manipulation, winemaker Kathy Malone gently leads the viticultural process in the distinct Naramata terroir. This premium growing area is still young and will only enhance with time—a trend she and her fans have already begun to witness. Her philosophy is that the fruit should shine through when drinking the wine, which means that the consumer will taste the effects of the soil, sun, and varietal instead of a heavy-handed winemaking method. Executive chef Rob Cordonier shares this philosophy and creates food at the bistro to enhance and accentuate the small-batch wines. He relies on local farmers for his produce, dairy, and meats, and makes those items the center of his menu. Following Kathy's philosophy, Rob knows that superior ingredients will help him create memorable dishes that reflect Hillside Winery & Bistro.

1350 Naramata Road, Penticton
250.493.6274 www.hillsidewinery.ca

Photographs: above and facing page by Mychaylo Prystupe; right by Stephanie Seaton

INNISKILLIN OKANAGAN

Inniskillin Okanagan is a globally respected pioneer in the wine industry. Committed to producing ultra-premium wines from only the best grapes grown in British Columbia, the estate winery has been shaping the Canadian winemaking landscape for more than 35 years.

In addition to a diverse portfolio of awarded table wines, Inniskillin Okanagan is renowned for its exceptional selection of icewines, which are produced during the extreme Canadian winter when the grapes freeze naturally on the vine at -8 degrees Celsius and are harvested frozen. Rich and concentrated, Inniskillin Okanagan Icewine is internationally awarded, recognized, and sought-after.

The winery shares a gorgeous wine boutique with Jackson-Triggs. Open year round, the space offers interactive wine tastings—including unique varietals and winery-only offerings—and memorable food and wine pairing experiences. Guests can enjoy and purchase a selection of wines in a number of tiers: Okanagan Estate, Reserve, Discovery, and Dark Horse Vineyard Series.

Winemaker Derek Kontkanen came to Inniskillin Okanagan just in time for the 2014 harvest. Derek won several awards at Jackson-Triggs Okanagan Estate, including Best Icewine in the World two years in a row by the International Wine & Spirits Competition in London. Continuing the legacy of Inniskillin Okanagan established by Sandor Mayer, Derek is delighted to add his creativity and expertise to the brand.

7857 Tucelnuit Drive, Oliver
250.498.4500 www.inniskillin.com

Photographs by Allison Kuhl Photography

JACKSON-TRIGGS

Jackson-Triggs is a blend of the founders' names, Allan Jackson and Don Triggs, who established the winery in 1993. With their partnership began an unwavering dedication to quality, value, and tradition, which the team continues to honour today. Surrounded in almost every direction by lakes, mountains, vineyards, and desert to the far south, Jackson-Triggs Okanagan wines are made from grapes harvested from some of the most beautiful and lush vineyards in the Okanagan Valley.

The Jackson-Triggs Okanagan portfolio includes table, sparkling, and icewine in various quality tiers; these include the SunRock collection of ultra-premium table wines sourced exclusively from the prestigious SunRock Vineyard site in Osoyoos. Grand Reserve and Reserve tiers each have a variety of wines—from bold varietals to smooth and easy drinking blends—to suit your need or occasion. Highly awarded winemaker Brooke Blair oversees all winemaking for the complete portfolio of Jackson-Triggs

Okanagan Estate wines. Open year round, the newly renovated Jackson-Triggs Okanagan Estate Tasting Gallery offers visitors and small groups a rare glimpse into the complete wine tasting experience including unique varietals and limited edition wines only found at the winery.

Jackson-Triggs is one of Canada's most awarded wineries and has been named Best Canadian Winery an unprecedented number of times in international and domestic competitions.

7857 Tucelnuit, Oliver
250.498.4500 www.jacksontriggswinery.com

Photographs by Allison Kuhl Photography

THE JOY OF LIVING CENTRE

Spectacular scenery, an invitation for total self-discovery, a mantra to enjoy the gift of life, and air that simply purrs. Here, there is a rare vibrational frequency that immediately helps you feel relaxed. You have arrived at The Joy of Living Centre. Housed in a gorgeous seven-bedroom villa, the centre is nestled among 40 mountainous acres in the Joe Rich Area. It is owned and operated by Joy Stewart, a woman full of light whose connection to the earth and understanding of the eternal inspires all who meet her.

The Joy of Living Centre offers a wide range of healthful, spiritually rejuvenating activities, from yoga and Reiki to hydrotherapy hot tub soaks. Joy personally leads a variety of enlightening workshops centering on mindfulness and integrating the personality with the soul. She believes that life needs to be lighter and wishes to the enrich body and soul of all who visit the centre and call it home, whether for a few hours or several days.

Throughout their stay, guests are pampered with organic gourmet cuisine, much of it grown onsite, and even invited to work in the gardens as a meditative exchange with nature. A creek meanders through the property, whose labyrinth, sacred woodlands, and fairy forest beg to be explored. Free-roaming sheep and nearby horse farms add to the setting's bucolic flair. Echoing the day's wonder-filled moments, evening time offers another special treat: a magical view of an earth-colored sunset against a backdrop of rugged mountains, in perfect harmony with the peacefulness of the land.

2770 Schram Road, Kelowna
250.807.2244 www.thejoyoflivingcentre.com

Photographs by Namara Joy

KELOWNA FLIGHTCRAFT

Flights of wine and airplane flights—both are involved in the origins of Kelowna Flightcraft, an aircraft maintenance and modification service. The company began when Joe Capozzi of Calona Wines, an avid pilot with a hangar where he built wine tanks, offered aircraft mechanic, Barry Lapointe, the opportunity to work out of his hangar. Eventually Barry and his business partner Jim Rogers took over the hangar and Kelowna Flightcraft was born.

With a worldwide clientele, the company flies commercial cargo, trains RCAF pilots, and maintains hundreds of aircraft annually. It prioritizes reliable, on-time service and the flexibility to answer any demand. While most Kelowna residents are unaware of what actually happens behind the hangar doors onsite at the facility, amid a friendly environment, technicians handle heavy aircraft maintenance, overhauls, modifications, paint, and plating.

Modifications include avionics; repairs and upgrades to major structures; and engine, landing gear, cargo door, winglet, and auxiliary fuel tank installations.

Kelowna Flightcraft accepts a wide array of opportunities, primarily based on word-of-mouth and a stellar reputation. With half a century of experience, the company is an Okanagan success story on the world stage.

5655 Airport Way, Kelowna
250.491.5500 www.flightcraft.ca

Photographs courtesy of Kelowna Flightcraft Ltd.

LA BUSSOLA RESTAURANT

The love of family and a passion for fine cuisine led Francesco Coccaro to travel the world in search of the perfect place to not only open his restaurant, but also to raise his family. Despite exploring several different locations, Francesco settled on Kelowna as the place to open La Bussola Restaurant in 1974. Together with his wife, chef Lauretta Coccaro, Francesco has created a warm, welcoming atmosphere for diners to enjoy Old World Italian favorites with a twist, such as Lauretta's gnocchi made from ricotta cheese instead of potato. Their son Luigi serves as general manager of the restaurant and holds a diploma in wine and spirits from the Wine and Spirit Education Trust. He is also a Certified Sommelier and loves to share his passion for wine with guests. Customized educational wine dinners, led by Luigi with guest winemakers from around the world, feature personalized menus and are a favorite among guests.

The Coccaros pay homage to their family's agricultural heritage back in Salerno, Italy, by approaching food in a garden-to-table manner. The bread is handmade daily and dishes feature vegetables grown from the restaurant's garden whenever possible. The wine collection dates back to bottles from the mid-'80s, and the restaurant offers special menus throughout the year.

1451 Ellis Street, Kelowna
250.763.3110 www.labussolarestaurant.com

Photographs by Glen Durrell Photography

LAKE BREEZE WINERY

A slice of Tuscany in the south central Okanagan Valley, the Mediterranean charm of Lake Breeze Winery is just as captivating as the Naramata Bench countryside that surrounds it. Located 15 minutes outside of Penticton, the destination was named for the glistening lake that borders it and the winds that blow across the bluffs year round.

Originally built in 1996, the picturesque winery has been called "the most beautifully situated winery on the entire Naramata Bench." The first grapevines at Lake Breeze were actually planted more than 10 years earlier, making them some of the most mature, and consequently robust, on the Naramata Bench. The current owners, the MacIntyre family, acquired the winery in 2001 and have since carefully grown the operation more than

threefold, now producing more than 10,000 cases of award-winning wine each year, using those original grapes and other superior fruit grown nearby.

Winemaker and president Garron Elmes, who originally hails from Capetown, South Africa, has been a part of the Lake Breeze journey since its very first days as an operating cellar. Focusing on the true character of each varietal, Garron endeavors to take the natural expression of the grape and transfer it to the bottle with as little intervention as possible. The result is a clean, crisp, and fruit-driven product—from the signature aromatic Pinot Blanc to the earthy Seven Poplars Pinot Noir.

Photograph courtesy of Lake Breeze

The bold nature of the wine encompasses not only the exceptional qualities of the Naramata Bench vines, but also its inherent connection to the property and the people who produce it.

Lake Breeze's intimate tasting room provides the opportunity to connect with other wine enthusiasts while exploring a range of new sips and mingling with the passionate team. In addition, visitors can savor a wine-paired lunch at The Patio at Lake Breeze, the property's renowned restaurant, featuring a rustic-chic ambience and scenic outdoor dining deck. Helmed by chef Mark Ashton, the menu is defined by enticing plates that artfully highlight the natural richness and full-bodied flavor of the freshest local ingredients from independent growers and artisans.

Photographs courtesy of Lake Breeze

Photograph courtesy of Lake Breeze

Combining their affinity of wine with an enthusiasm for the local community, Lake Breeze also participates in a number of charitable initiatives and events, donating tasting fees and bottles for such causes as the South Okanagan-Similkameen Conservation Program, Penticton & District Community Resource Society, and South Okanagan Women in Need Society.

930 Sammet Road, Naramata
250.496.5659 www.lakebreeze.ca

Photographs courtesy of Lake Breeze

LAKE OKANAGAN RESORT

Lake Okanagan Resort is an invitation to leave the frenzy of the city behind, in favor of a picturesque retreat. The mountainside oasis offers year-round outdoor adventures, romantic getaways, corporate retreats, wedding packages, and memorable family vacations on 300 acres of parkland along the western shore of Okanagan Lake.

Located just 20 minutes from downtown Kelowna, the resort is convenient yet feels like a million miles away. Guests can unwind at their choice of venues, including three outdoor swimming pools, two hot tubs, a lit tennis court, a nine-hole executive golf course, or the Beyond Wrapture Day Spa. Interpretive hiking trails offer the chance to explore the beautiful surroundings, yet lake views may be taken in from all points of the property.

Guests enjoy indulging at the on-site Vantage Pointe Restaurant as well as the Poolside Barefoot Bar, which are open seasonally. Culinary enthusiasts can whip up their own masterpieces in the private en-suite kitchen facilities or outdoor barbecue areas. The resort also includes a convenience store as well as a full-service marina with boat fuel.

2751 Westside Road, Kelowna
250.769.3511 www.lakeokanagan.com

Photographs courtesy of Lake Okanagan Resort

LANG VINEYARDS

As one of British Columbia's original wineries, Lang Vineyards prides itself on building the local wine region that was once unknown. Upon immigrating to Canada in 1980, German couple Guenther and Kristina Lang purchased the property because of its ideal microclimate. Guenther envisioned a land one day filled with grapevines and dotted with wineries—little did he know, he was on to something big. Lang Vineyards opened for business in 1990 and has helped push South Okanagan's viticultural movement forward, aiding in the removal of restrictive laws for small-acreage wineries, or farm gate wineries as they were termed. This ultimately led to the creation of the Farm Gate License; a legislative move that opened doors to area growers and attracted vintners from around the globe. The area flourished.

Newly renovated, the wine shop and tasting room offer enough space for large groups to enjoy the facilities yet maintains a feeling of intimacy for couples who want something a little quieter. With six-and-a-half acres of land sitting high on the Naramata Bench, Lang Vineyards takes advantage of both the sweeping views and premium terroir. Grapes are never imported; everything is grown locally. Aged in stainless steel tanks and oak casks to highlight the fruit's flavor, the wine is primarily comprised of vinifera varietals, including pinot auxerrois, gewürztraminer, riesling, pinot noir, merlot, and pinot meunier. Marechal Foch is a hybrid that is their signature red, and remains one of the most popular wines since its first vintage in 1989.

2493 Gammon Road, Naramata
778.514.5598 www.langvineyards.ca

Photographs: top by C.W. Seer Photography; middle, bottom, and facing page by Virtual BC Tours

MANTEO RESORT WATERFRONT HOTEL & VILLAS AND SMACK DAB RESTAURANT

If you think one resort can't have it all, then you haven't visited **Manteo Resort Waterfront Hotel & Villas**. It's a year-round resort offering first-class accommodations on the shores of beautiful Okanagan Lake. The peaceful location is just minutes away from championship golf courses, wineries, hiking, ski slopes, and boutique shops, as well as the best attractions on the lake: waterskiing, kayaking, paddle boarding, and boating. The resort provides easy access to downtown attractions, nightlife, and the Kelowna International Airport. Accommodations range from intimate guestrooms, to one-bedroom suites, to spacious two- and three-bedroom villas; every room has a private balcony, flat-screen television, luxurious bedding, and stunning garden, mountain, or lake views. The villas include private living rooms, gas fireplaces, fully equipped kitchens, and patios with personal barbecues. Because of its wide range of choices in accommodation size and style, the resort suits families, couples, and business travelers. Manteo Resort features numerous amenities including indoor and outdoor pools and hot tubs, fitness centre, big screen movie theater, kids waterslide and spray park, tennis court, nine-hole putting green, private beach, and 5,000 square feet of meeting space.

Manteo's on-site restaurant **Smack DAB** is aptly named for its scenic location, smack dab on the edge of the lake. The swanky kitchen and bar boasts "crazy good food" and is open for breakfast buffet, lunch, and dinner. The clever open-concept interior design allows patrons to chat with friends and take in views of the lake while watching the chefs work their magic at the forno oven. A wall of glass doors provides an open-air experience during the summer and unobstructed views the rest of the year. Pleasant weather draws guests outside to the expansive, 150-seat lakeside patio for casual fine dining at its best. Private groups are welcome to reserve The View Room, where signature views and a handcrafted dining table establish the ambience and a full setup of audiovisual equipment supports the needs of business and social gatherings of all sorts. Whether enjoying a full meal

or just stopping in for a drink, Smack DAB is a premier culinary destination. Its menu, which includes wildly fun originals and tried-and-true favorites with a twist, invites you to "say hello to your taste buds one at a time." To complement its cuisine, Smack DAB proudly serves Kelowna's largest selection of locally crafted beer, a great local wine list, and crafty cocktails.

3762 Lakeshore Road, Kelowna
800.445.5255 www.manteo.com

Photographs courtesy of Manteo Resort Waterfront Hotel & Villas

MONASHEE ADVENTURE TOURS

There is no better way to see southern British Columbia than by bike—and there's no better man to lead you than Ed Kruger, or Trailhead Ed as he's commonly called. A natural-born biker, Ed has been riding almost as long as he could walk, so it seemed only natural that his career path was on a bike. Starting Monashee Adventure Tours in 1991, Ed has come a long way since riding his childhood Motocross look-alike; but he's still having just as much fun.

As a native to Kelowna, Ed takes pride in showing off the region's natural beauty. Ed and his team offer visitors a variety of tours that can accommodate any group. For a relaxing, laid back ride with regional commentary, riders will enjoy the Kelowna Historical Bike, which includes a flat two-hour tour with local history. The tour features lake views, beach breaks, and trails through Knox Mountain. A pedi-cab tour of Myra Canyon is the newest addition, perfect for families with children, senior citizens, and mobility

impaired guests. Customized road cycling tours are available with route planning, van transportation, and support service. For groups that want tailored tours, the Kettle Valley Tour offers school outings, which include a stop off for a barbecue meal; or winery excursions to nearby vineyards like Tantalus Winery and Summerhill Pyramid Winery. Touring by bike gives visitors an opportunity to see the countryside just as Ed sees it, up close and firsthand.

1591 Highland Drive North, Kelowna
250.762.9253 www.monasheeadventuretours.com

Photographs courtesy of Monashee Adventure Tours

MT. BOUCHERIE WINERY

Love of the planting is our true passion - assisting the vines to grow, and watching the raw grapes become wine. Our enthusiasm is as robust as the premier fruit and award-winning sips that we produce here at Mt. Boucherie Winery in Lakeview Heights. Mt. Boucherie has evolved from a master grape grower into one of British Columbia's premier wineries.. We derive our name from one of West Kelowna's dramatic landmark mountains—the

remnant of a former volcano—that overlooks the vineyards from the west.

Our roots run deep. We have been here since the beginning of the Okanagan wine industry and we are proud to own and manage some of the oldest vineyards in the valley. Since 1968, Mt. Boucherie has grown the finest Vinifera grapes in British Columbia and currently owns approximately

200 acres (80.93 ha) of vineyards located in Cawston (Similkameen Valley), Oliver's (Golden Mile), Okanagan Falls and West Kelowna. The primary goal at our 20,000-square-foot processing, fermentation, and bottling facility is to create consistently high-caliber wines, which all bear the BC Vintners Quality Alliance certification. Our wines are incredibly food-friendly, and the varities of wine available ensures there is a bottle to match your palate, plate and mood. The unique qualities of our wines are developed through our passion for the region and for producing top wines that reflect the diversity of our vineyards' terroir.

Photograph by Lionel Trudel

Indeed, winemaker Jim Faulkner, is zealous about highlighting the integrity of the grape. "Everything starts with great quality fruit, and here Mt. Boucherie shines," says Jim. "There is an unmatched level of consistency. It certainly makes my job a lot easier."

The Mt. Boucherie philosophy is straightforward: Keep it simple and let the grapes speak for themselves. But the wine tells a far more complex story; it's a layered, exceptional experience that celebrates the region and includes some uncommon varietals including zweigelt and blaufränkisch, cold-climate whites, along with pinot noir icewines and the Alsatian varietals of riesling, gewürztraminer, and ehrenfelser. It has been our long-time goal of using 100-percent estate-grown grapes from our own vineyard holdings.

Photographs by Lionel Trudel

Photograph by Lionel Trudel

Likewise, the winery itself is a veritable celebration for the senses, with exquisite views of the surrounding valley and vineyards to accompany daily wine tastings. The picnic deck, overlooking Okanagan Lake, provides the perfect afternoon respite, especially when paired with a glass of wine. As a leader in the vibrant and distinctive Okanagan wine industry, Mt. Boucherie truly encompasses the complete wine journey—from vine to bottle.

829 Douglas Road, Kelowna
877.684.2748 www.mtboucheriewinery.com

Photographs by Lionel Trudel

NK'MIP CELLARS

Nk'Mip Cellars is the first Aboriginal owned and operated winery in North America. This partnership between Constellation Brands Canada and the Osoyoos Indian Band has resulted in an award-winning lakeside winery. Situated in Canada's only pocket desert, the winery offers some of the most spectacular views in the Okanagan.

The Nk'Mip winemaking team is stacked with talent and includes winemaker Randy Picton, assistant winemaker Justin Hall, and cellar supervisor Aaron Crey. In 2002 under Randy's direction, Nk'Mip introduced a series of reserve wines labeled Qwam Qwmt that have received numerous "Best of Class," platinum, double gold, and gold awards from international competitions. For the 2014 WineAlign National Wine Awards, Nk'Mip earned medals for all 14 of the wines it submitted and was ranked the third best winery in Canada.

Visitors to the winery can choose from wine shop tastings and winery tours that highlight the winery's heritage and commitment to quality. The gorgeous, high ceilings and First Nations décor offer a unique and inspired setting in which to enjoy views, history, delicious wines, and a unique selection of local Aboriginal artisan merchandise and culinary treats.

The seasonal Patio Restaurant is a beautiful place to grab a table and enjoy the breathtaking view while sampling locally sourced gourmet cuisine and award-winning Nk'Mip wines. Everything is handcrafted using premium local ingredients. The Patio comes to life in the spring and is open for lunch daily from April through October.

1400 Rancher Creek Road, Osoyoos
250.495.2985 www.nkmipcellars.com

Photographs by Allison Kuhl Photography

OKANAGAN LODGING COMPANY

With luxury rental properties in some of the finest destinations throughout the Okanagan Valley, Okanagan Lodging Company provides a distinct basecamp for a Kelowna dream getaway. Breathtaking views are assured at any of the company's family-sized homes brimming with amenities including central pools, hot tubs, game and exercise rooms, and even rooftop decks, all with convenient access to the area's world-class golf courses, sparkling lakes, biking and hiking trails, superior ski slopes, and destination wineries.

Okanagan Lodging Company's flagship community, Mission Shores, is located in Kelowna's prestigious Lower Mission neighborhood and features sophisticated cottage-style living along the sublime natural beachfront of Okanagan Lake. This fabulous location offers easy access to the Greenway Trail, beaches, the Pandosy shopping district, and beautiful Okanagan Lake. The property has boat moorage available, all on electric lifts.

Another of Okanagan Lodging Company's offerings, the Vintage Collection, boasts private homes in premier spots across the valley—steps from the waterfront, the fairway, the orchard, or the vineyard—for the ultimate vacation dream come true.

600-3880 Truswell Road, Kelowna
866.448.7829 www.okanaganlodging.com

Photographs: top and bottom courtesy of Okanagan Lodging Company; middle and facing page by The Mission Group

OKANAGAN SPIRITS
CRAFT DISTILLERY

Inspired by British Columbia's natural bounty, Okanagan Spirits Craft Distillery has used the region's fruits and grains as its source for liqueurs, vodka, whisky, gin, absinthe, brandies, and more. Handcrafted in copper pot stills under the direction of master distiller Peter von Hahn, the spirits at Okanagan Spirits have received international acclaim, and once you know the process it's easy to understand why. Free from colouring, preservatives, and all things artificial, the product is made solely from local crops, which yield a pure, unparalleled flavour. Raspberry Liqueur, Poire Williams, Italian Prune, Sea Buckthorn, and even Taboo Genuine Absinthe—made from botanicals of anise, lemon balm hyssop, fennel, petite wormwood, and grande wormwood—are a few of the award-winning selections featured on the Okanagan Spirits menu.

Recognized by World Spirits as a world-class distillery, the distillery offers visitors as much education as it does flavour. Facility tours give guests insight into the art of the craft, revealing details of the process and letting them see the careful procedures firsthand. Tours are available year-round at both locations and end with a rewarding stop by the tasting bar.

Kelowna | Vernon
888.292.5270 www.okanaganspirits.com

Photographs: above, left, and facing page bottom by Shawn Talbot Photography; facing page top by Jeremie Dyck

ORCHARD PARK SHOPPING CENTRE

The '70s had just begun when Orchard Park Shopping Centre first opened its doors on September 28, 1971. Appropriately named after the original expanse of orchards that formerly occupied the property, it included two big name stores at the time, Sears and The Bay, as well as 35 smaller retail shops. Orchard Park's prime Okanagan Valley locale, near bustling Harvey Avenue, makes it a high-traffic destination. The centre is now the largest shopping mall that lies between Calgary and Vancouver with more than 700,000 square feet of retail space.

There are nearly 200 various stores and services at Orchard Park, which touts exclusive shops to the area like Old Navy, Sephora, BCBG Max Azria, Pseudio, Aerie and Pandora. Other popular highlights include Chapters—equipped with a Starbucks, of course—Sport Chek and the mall's original cornerstones, Sears and The Bay, which remain prominent. Orchard Park's Guest Services Team can provide shoppers with detailed tourism information, there is a fully-equipped parenting room for guests with small children, a 500 seat food court and various tea and coffee shops throughout the centre. Orchard Park even offers free space to non-profit organizations 10 months out of the year to support the local community, making it a unique and cultured destination for locals and visitors alike.

2271 Harvey Avenue Kelowna
800.610.7467 www.orchardparkshopping.com
Photographs by Sharla Pike Photography

PEACHES LINGERIE

Confidence is beautiful. That's something that Christina Conquergood, owner of Peaches Lingerie, knows for certain. After 20 years in the banking industry, Christina purchased, rebranded, and reinvented the chic boutique with the small town attention to detail in order to help women see themselves as the beautiful individuals they are. From the French vanilla, copper, and sleek black interiors to the spacious changing rooms based on customers' needs, Peaches Lingerie offers personalized service to every woman who walks in the door. Staff members that span every age demographic are ready to assist girls and women with custom bra fittings and one-on-one service that ensures absolute comfort with both the products offered and the fitter herself.

From spicy lingerie that guests can find in an old walk-in bank vault—what happens in the vault stays in the vault, they like to say—to Canadian-made

IF YOU ARE *confident*
YOU ARE *beautiful*

maternity wear and nursing bras that can be found in a room set aside solely for mothers-to-be, Peaches Lingerie has something for everyone. Their bra selection is amazing, from sizes 28C to 46J. Christina further promotes women by sponsoring women's sports teams including a minor hockey U18 girl's team and a women's soccer team. She's also heavily involved in many local charities in an effort to make the world a better place.

262 Main Street, Penticton
250.770.8308 www.peacheslingerie.com

Photographs by Cheline Lacroix

PENTICTON, BRITISH COLUMBIA

Voted one of the Top 10 Travel Destinations for 2012, Penticton is nestled between the golden sandy beaches of Okanagan and Skaha Lakes, in the interior of beautiful British Columbia. Known for its long hot summers and mild winters, Penticton has been a holiday play ground for many years and is considered the destination of choice in the Pacific Northwest.

It is highly regarded for its stunning natural beauty including mountains and lakes, but is also renowned for its organic farming methods which offer up an endless array of produce farms, fruit orchards, and vineyards, most of which are open to the public throughout the season. Indeed, Penticton is the hub of wine tourism in the Okanagan Valley providing direct access to more than 88 boutique wineries—60 wineries within a 20 minutes' drive of downtown—and is also the gateway to the stunning and world famous vineyards of the Naramata Bench.

Photographs by Melissa Barnes

WINE TASTING

*Photographs: facing page by Darryl Leniuk; top left by Andrea Johnson;
bottom left by Melissa Barnes*

As you would expect with so much natural beauty, Penticton offers a multitude of recreational activities. Whether it's skiing at Apex Mountain Resort, boating and fishing on the twin lakes, golfing the area's many courses, hiking and biking the Kettle Valley Trail, not to mention rock climbing at Skaha Bluffs, outdoor enthusiasts are sure to be busy. Penticton is also home to the world champion BCHL hockey team Penticton Vees who play throughout the winter months, as well as the PCSL soccer team Penticton Pinnacles, who play from May until July.

An already well-developed arts and social scene is being augmented with new events, restaurants, and accommodations. Penticton has more festivals and events than any other location in the wider region, meaning people now not only come for the peaches, beaches, wine tasting, and dining, but also to attend concerts and appreciate the arts generally.

With a fantastic climate, beautiful beaches, endless activities, and loads of festivals and events throughout the year, Penticton has something for everyone!

317 Martin Street, Penticton
250.809.8556
www.thepentictonhospitalityassociation.com

Photographs: left by Jason Dziver; top by Andrea Johnson; facing page by Melissa Barnes

PERSEUS WINERY

The philosophy at Perseus Winery is simple: good grapes equal good wine. The goal is to produce wines of character and distinction from some of British Columbia's finest terroirs. Grapes are sourced from the winery's estate vineyards—Lower Bench Vineyard in Naramata and Sunrise Vineyard in West Kelowna—as well as from renowned growers who farm in some of the most famous locations in both the Similkameen and Okanagan Valleys. These include, but are not limited to, Silver Barrel Vineyard overlooking Skaha Lake, Blind Creek Vineyard in Cawston, and Inkameep Vineyards in Oliver.

Visitors can enjoy sampling the wines at Perseus' main house—a charming mid-century home that has been renovated into an open, welcoming gathering place for wine enthusiasts. A tasting bar lets guests experience the wines and ask questions to the well-educated Perseus team while enjoying the beautifully re-purposed space. Private tasting experiences are also on offer for those looking for a more in-depth experience of the wines and regions of the valley. For those looking for a bite to eat, Perseus offers great picnic food options showcasing local food suppliers and artisans. The wines, food, view, and charm all make Perseus a great first stop on the gorgeous Naramata Bench.

134 Lower Bench Road, Penticton
250.490.8829 www.perseuswinery.com

Photographs: top and left by Mica Knibbs; right by Lionel Trudel

PLANET BEE HONEY FARM & HONEYMOON MEADERY

Ever heard of the Honeybee Olympics? Edwin Nowek's honeybees are gold medalists, their creations garnering top honors at the British Columbia festival. Since 1969, Ed has been enamored with the beauty and wonder of bees, practicing the art of beekeeping and advocating the myriad benefits that bees offer to our health, well-being, and the ecosystem as a whole. Planet Bee Honey Farm & Honeymoon Meadery is the culmination of his life's passion.

It's a magical place to visit. Whether you stop by to pick up some of Planet Bee's locally made products—delicious honey, healthful pollen, natural skincare items, beeswax candles, or acclaimed Honeymoon Mead—you're sure to leave with more than mere things. Ed, his son James, and their Planet Bee team aim to impart a deep love and respect for their marvelous creatures. All of the team members are enthusiastic about sharing their vast knowledge of the natural treasures of the honeybee hive. They invite visitors of all ages to experience the glass observatory, tour the apiary, and sample more than a dozen varieties of honey.

Adults appreciate learning about and tasting Honeymoon Mead—Planet Bee's honey wine, created at the onsite meadery. An alcoholic beverage of ancient significance, mead is made from fermented honey and water, often flavored with additional fruits, herbs, and spices. It is a delightfully diverse drink that ranges from dry to extremely sweet and can be served hot, cold, or slightly chilled. Mead is certainly a point of fascination for visitors and something for which Planet Bee has become quite famous.

As professional beekeepers, Ed and his team are focused not only on caring for their bees and creating wonderful products for people to enjoy, they also provide pollination services to local farms. Planet Bee serves a noble purpose and is a requisite part of Canada's flourishing agri-tourism industry.

5011 Bella Vista Road, Vernon
250.542.8088 www.planetbee.com

Photographs courtesy of Planet Bee Honey Farm & Honeymoon Meadery

POPLAR GROVE WINERY

Great wines are born from the courage to go beyond what is possible. One of the original five wineries on the Naramata Bench, Poplar Grove was founded in 1993. Over the past two decades, the team at Poplar Grove has worked with their estate vineyards to nurture potential into each bottle. The winery has grown into an international, award-winning producer of five core varietals: pinot gris, chardonnay, cabernet Franc, syrah, merlot, and a signature blend aptly named The Legacy. Throughout the years, Poplar Grove owner, Tony Holler, has found it takes courage to make the right choices in the vineyards, and collective patience to wait for nature to fully develop the grapes on the vines. At Poplar Grove, the process is not rushed; the red wines are kept in the winery cellar for a minimum of three years before they are available, ensuring that they are properly aged and ready to enjoy when released.

In 2011, the doors to Poplar Grove's brand new winery opened. Surrounded by estate vineyards and tucked into the southwest side of Munson Mountain,

Tony Holler, Owner and President

Andrew Holler, Penticton Vineyard Manager

the new winery and expansive tasting room allows guests to experience breathtaking views of the Okanagan Valley while sipping on a selection of Poplar Grove's signature wines. The new location is also home to a wine production facility, a showcase barrel hall, and the year-round, destination restaurant, the Vanilla Pod. Guests are invited to stay for lunch, dinner, or afternoon tapas to experience fresh and seasonal local ingredients perfectly paired with Poplar Grove's award-winning wines. A beneficial way to join the winemaking journey is to become a member of the Poplar Grove Wine Club. Members enjoy access to exclusive member-only wines, discounts on direct wine purchases, and invitations to annual winery parties. For wine enthusiasts from around the globe, this is the place to get a vivid taste of what the Okanagan Valley's Naramata Bench can deliver.

425 Middle Bench Road North, Penticton
250.493.9463 www.poplargrove.ca
Photographs by Andrew Topham

PRESTIGE HOTELS & RESORTS

Ranging from a stunning oceanfront resort in Greater Victoria to unique properties spread across the British Columbian landscape, Prestige Hotels & Resorts prides itself on providing exceptional services at an affordable price. Prestige would not exist today without the hard work and dedication of its founder, Joe Huber Sr. As a European immigrant who came to Canada with only 20 dollars in his pocket, Joe was able to thrive in his adopted country, working his way up from cabinetmaker to carpenter to eventually owning and operating his own motel business. With the support of his wife Anna and the help of his children, the business flourished. Joe was able to purchase a large property on Highway 97 and Abbott Street in Kelowna, a property that would become the first hotel in the Prestige franchise. Thanks to the ambition and vision of the founder, his son Joe Huber Jr., and his son-in-law Terry Schneider, the modest motel business has grown into an upscale hotel chain. With locations in the Okanagan, Kootenay Rockies, and on Vancouver Island, Prestige Hotels & Resorts continues to offer a unique regional experience. The friendly and knowledgeable staff honor the hotel's legacy by providing guests with an unforgettable stay.

Corporate Office: 1635 Abbott Street, Suite 102, Kelowna
877.737.8443 www.prestigehotelsandresorts.com

Photographs courtesy of Prestige Oceanfront Resort

QUAILS' GATE WINERY

Recognized internationally and nationally as one of the country's top agri-tourism sites, Quails' Gate offers more than 200 acres of vineyards. The winery is considered to be a leader in the development of viticulture practices in Canada, as well as a benchmark for pinot noir.

Its illustrious history dates back to 1908 when Richard Stewart Sr. settled in the Okanagan Valley in 1908 and founded one of the area's most successful nursery businesses. In 1956, Richard's son, Dick, purchased the estate property knowing that it was potentially one of the best sites in the Okanagan Valley for premium grape production. Five years later the first vinifera wines were planted, which led to the family's discovery of its passion for winemaking. In 1989, Ben and Ruth Stewart founded Quails' Gate winery and began the family's transition into the winery business. From there, the entire family joined together in the pursuit of making Quails' Gate winery one of Canada's foremost producers of premium VQA wines.

Today Quails' Gate wines fully express their place of origin, as they are crisp, fresh, fruit-forward, rich in color, and intense in flavor. Through years of extensive research, the Stewarts have found that the unique qualities of their vineyards express themselves in the glass, making Quails' Gate wines a true reflection of terroir.

3303 Boucherie Road, West Kelowna
250.769.4451 www.quailsgate.com

Photographs courtesy of Quails' Gate Winery

SANDHILL WINERY

At Sandhill, it's all about the single vineyard philosophy. Each bottle of Sandhill wine is made from grapes that come from one of six unique BC vineyards, and each vineyard possesses a unique combination of soil composition, slope, sun exposure, and drainage. In addition, each vineyard manager employs techniques that bring subtle influences into the growing environment, so it's inevitable that Sandhill's grapes offer unique characteristics in every vintage.

Master Winemaker Howard Soon founded Sandhill in 1997 with the idea of showing a premium expression and giving credit to the people who grow the grapes. On every bottle of Sandhill you'll find Howard's signature, as well as the grape grower's. A pioneer in the British Columbia wine industry, Howard became the first winemaker in history to receive all three top honours at the 2009 Wine Access Canadian Wine Awards, where Sandhill won for Best Red Wine of the Year, Best White Wine of the Year and Winery of the Year.

In May 2014, Sandhill opened its renovated urban winery in downtown Kelowna. The modern 8,000-square-foot space features a large glacier sculpture that pays homage to the Okanagan Valley's natural geological features and glacial history, which give the region its ideal grape-growing conditions. With vineyards ranging from the Naramata Bench all the way down to the Similkameen Valley, Sandhill carefully nurtures its relationship with the land to produce vibrantly fresh wines with strong fruit character.

1125 Richter Street, Kelowna
250.762.9144 www.sandhillwines.ca

Photographs: top, bottom middle, and facing page by Joseph Chan, Steven Chan/ARTiculation Group, Toronto; above and top middle by Chris Gardiner

SEE YA LATER RANCH WINERY

Perched on Hawthorne Mountain, almost 1,900 feet above sea level overlooking Skaha Lake, See Ya Later Ranch Winery offers one of the most picturesque landscapes in the Okanagan Valley. The winery is steeped in local history surrounding the lively legacy of Major Hugh Fraser, a colourful character who purchased the property in 1919. He planted vines and seeded a legend that has become the winery's namesake. The major's London-raised wife was not pleased with the rustic atmosphere of her new home—she left the valley and a three-word note: "see ya later."

The major's love for dogs lives on in the extremely dog-friendly winery. The "barking lot" offers your pooches a place to relax while you enjoy a delicious lunch on the patio.

The winery location couldn't be more ideal for growing premium grapes; the vineyard's slope, proximity to the lake, warm days, and cool evenings encourage healthy ripening of cool weather varietals including pinot noir and close to 50 acres of gewürztraminer.

Additionally, the portfolio features amazing blends named after some of the major's favorite companions, "Rover" Shiraz-Viognier and "Ping" Meritage.

Winemaker Dave Carson is a bit of an Okanagan legend himself, having worked at local vineyards since he was just 11 years old. As the senior winemaker he is responsible for managing the cellar and creating a portfolio of wines inspired by this seriously playful brand.

Open 11 months of the year, the winery is particularly breathtaking mid-May through late September when lunch is served on the gorgeous outdoor deck. With unparalleled views, See Ya Later Ranch offers a spectacular backdrop for outdoor and special events for up to 225 guests.

2575 Green Lake Road, Okanagan Falls
250.497.8267 www.sylranch.com

Photographs: top, facing page bottom left, bottom right by Allison Kuhl: facing page top right by Tim Kelly, BrandFX

SYL

DOG AND
OWNER
CROSSING

SEEYA
LATER
RANCH

SEVEN STONES WINERY

Passion, hard work, and a dedication to the land; these are the values that winery owners have always held sacred. The same can be said of George Hanson, owner and winemaker of Seven Stones Winery located in beautiful Similkameen Valley. Under George's careful direction, Seven Stones—named for the seven rock formations throughout the region—not only produces exquisite wines reflective of the terroir, it's also a destination that looks like it's straight out of a fairytale. The picturesque vineyards stretch toward majestic Mount Chopaka in the distance. Visitors love to bring a picnic lunch and enjoy the spectacular vistas from the observation deck. A nearby gazebo with a spiral staircase leads down to the wine cave below,

where the estate-grown varietals of chardonnay, pinot noir, merlot, and more are stored using the natural cool environment provided by the earth.

The cave was designed by Vivianne, whom George met and married a few years after the first planting of the vineyard. She shared his passion for fine wine and could often be found visiting with guests or coordinating the behind-the-scenes activities of the winery. She always had a smile on her face for guests, even as she battled ovarian cancer. After her passing, George came across a note she'd left, outlining her wishes for the wine cave. George and Vivianne's eldest son Colin—who had already begun

working on the plans for the cave—cross-referenced this document with their own plans and made modifications in order to construct the wine cave to her wishes. When visitors step foot into the wine cave, they aren't just stepping into a storage area burrowed into the earth. They're stepping into a revered memorial of a loving and supportive partner.

And that personal presence is everywhere at this quaint winery. George's home—which was designed by Vivianne—sits about 75 feet from the small tasting room. George himself is involved in every part of the winemaking process. In the intimate tasting room, guests not only sample wines,

but may also shop for a piece of jewelry to commemorate their trip. The offshoot business was one of Vivianne's passions, and so the tasting room still features these little luxurious treasures.

1143 Highway #3, Cawston
250.499.2144 www.sevenstones.ca

Photograph by Sian James

Photographs by Sian James

Photographs by Sian James

THE RESIDENCES AT SPIRIT RIDGE

A veritable oasis in Canada's only desert, Bellstar's latest development The Residences at Spirit Ridge are vacation rental villas nestled on a sun-drenched hillside overlooking the crystal blue waters of Osoyoos Lake and the Sonora Golf Course. Mountains, orchards and miles of rolling vineyards surround the villas earning the region its "Napa of the North" designation. The Residences are part of a larger resort complex which features Nk'Mip Cellars and the neighbouring Nk'Mip Desert Cultural Centre, offering guests the opportunity to learn about the local Aboriginal winery as well as the history of the valley and its first inhabitants.

While the vibrant cultural connection is palpable at The Residences at Spirit Ridge, so too is a feeling of immense luxury. Spacious, condo-style all-suite accommodations set the tone for The Residences, featuring large walkouts to patios featuring barbecues and gas fireplaces offering a lush alfresco option in Canada's warmest city. Venturing outside your villa yields additional indulgences—from family-friendly pools at the main resort, to a stroll along the property's private beach, or even a rejuvenating treatment at the Solterra Desert Spa.

#23 8000 Valleyview Drive, Osoyoos
877.313.9463 www.spiritridgeresidences.com

Photographs courtesy of Bellstar Hotels & Resorts pg 104

Photograph by Sihawn Talbot, pg 105

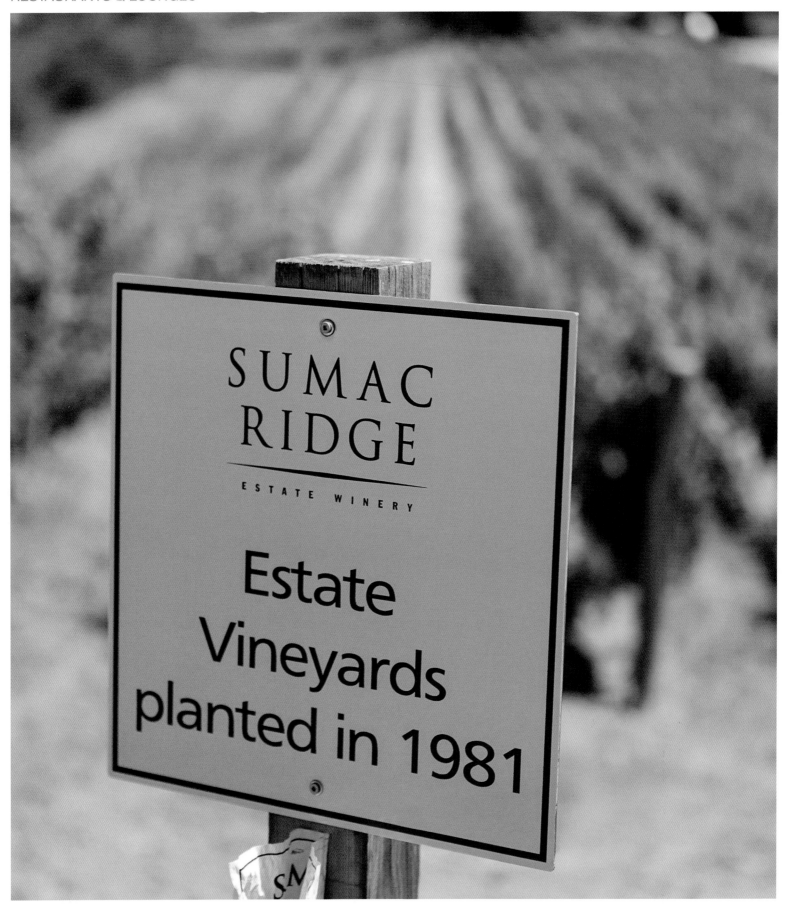

SUMAC RIDGE ESTATE WINERY

Founded in 1979, Sumac Ridge Estate Winery is the oldest operating estate winery in British Columbia and has been dedicated to producing 100-percent British Columbia grown wines since its inception. Nestled in the heart of the Okanagan Valley in the scenic town of Summerland, Sumac Ridge is known for its team's passion, innovation, and commitment to quality. With a magnificent setting and great service, guests feel relaxed and welcome.

At Sumac Ridge Estate Winery, three brands stand tall with distinct and engaging environments in one iconic location: Sumac Ridge, Black Sage, and Steller's Jay. Summer and fall are particularly gorgeous times to visit, yet the winery is open year-round for tours, tastings, and special events.

The wine shop features contemporary tasting bars and sophisticated décor anchored by Sumac Ridge's familiar and approachable wines. The food-friendly wines make visitors want to visit around the dinner table or cozy up with a

good book. Perhaps best known for the crowd pleasing gewürztraminer, Sumac Ridge also boasts delightful whites including unoaked chardonnay, sauvignon blanc, and pinot grigo. Its reds include cabernet-merlot, merlot, pinot noir, and a limited-edition, robust, mouthwatering shiraz.

The effervescent and playful Steller's Jay experience celebrates the best of BC sparkling wine with Steller's Jay Brut and Pinnacle. Guests can visit the sparkling wine cave and savour the signature truffle popcorn paired with delicious traditional-method bubbles. These fine champagne style sparkling wines are well-respected and perfect for any occasion.

The strong and masculine Black Sage Vineyard environment speaks to the bold wines produced from the tenacious 20-year-old vines of the South Okanagan's Black Sage Vineyard. Winemaker Jason James produces juicy, intensely flavoured wines—including merlot, cabernet Franc, and cabernet sauvignon—and visitors also appreciate the exclusive offerings of shiraz and zinfandel. In fact, Jason is the man behind all the wines of Sumac Ridge, Steller's Jay, and Black Sage Vineyard. From tasting barrel samples to the organized chaos of crush, the passionate winemaker enjoys the entire process.

The winery also offers two exclusive rooms: the sleek and stylish Black Sage Vineyard Hall, ideal for private events, and the Steller's Jay Sparkling Wine Cave, which is accessible through paid tours and special experiences.

Approachable, enjoyable, and offering a little something special, the various environments at Sumac Ridge perfectly showcase—label by label—all that this impressive estate has to offer.

17403 Highway 97N, Summerland
250.494.0451 www.sumacridge.com
www.blacksagevineyard.com

Photographs: right by Tim Kelly, BrandFX;
facing page by Allison Kuhl Photography

URBAN DISTILLERIES

When Mike Urban launched his namesake Urban Distilleries in 2010, the former circuit board designer smartly branded his premier collection of handcrafted spirits after one of British Columbia's rarest symbols. Known for their all-white fur, "spirit bears"—properly known as Kermode bears—are actually a sub-species of the North American black bear. Only a tenth of the black bear population possesses the rare recessive gene that results in the snowy hair color.

In the span of just a few years, Mike's carefully concocted recipes, which are all natural and gluten free, have earned him both local and global recognition. Urban Distilleries produces Spirit Bear vodka, gin and espresso-infused vodka as well as the Urban single malt whisky and Grappa Moscato.

His longtime passion for distilling was spurred on by a visit to the Camus Cognac Distillery in France. After much research and preparation, Mike made it official and shipped in customized stills from Germany.

As British Columbia's first-ever legal craft artisan distillery, Mike's distillery became a local treasure, just like the spirit bear. In fact, Urban Distilleries assists in efforts to protect the spirit bear by donating partial proceeds as well as all funds from distillery tastings toward the Spirit Bear Youth Coalition, a youth-led environmental organization. Mike's unique edge, his drive for perfection, and an earnest community focus help Urban Distilleries continue to set the standard for handcrafted spirits with local flair.

325 Bay Avenue, Kelowna
778.478.0939 www.urbandistilleries.ca

Photographs by Darren Hull Studios

CATHEDRAL LAKES LODGE

Not a single television or radio can be found at Cathedral Lakes Lodge—a rare occurrence in today's modern world, but one that the full-service hiking and fishing wilderness destination values. The lodge, built in 1972 in Cathedral Provincial Park, is situated at 2,000 metres above sea level next to Quiniscoe Lake. A stone fireplace is the main feature in the cozy lounge of the two-storey lodge, which also offers guest rooms, a hot tub, and a dining room. In addition to homemade buffet-style meals, the chef will cook up your catch if you hook a fish in any of the park's pristine, turquoise-coloured lakes.

More than 33,000 hectares comprise the park, home to abundant wildlife and awe-inspiring scenery. The Cathedral Rim Trail attracts hikers from around the world for its 360-degree views of the North Cascade and Coastal and Okanagan mountain ranges. The park's towering rock formations with names such as The Giant Cleft and Smokey the Bear are a must-see.

Quaint cabins, photography workshops, painting classes, wine tastings, and more contribute to an authentic adventure at Cathedral Lakes Lodge. After all, without TV and phones, a serene lakeside sunset is best enjoyed in peace.

Located near Keremeos
888.CLL.HIKE (255.4454) www.cathedrallakes.ca

Photographs by ET2media

CHRISTINA LAKE GOLF CLUB

When a golf course is beautiful enough to attract those who have never even picked up a club, you know the designer did something very right. Indeed, famed course architect Les Furber created some his finest holes at Christina Lake Golf Club. Entertaining for new players yet still challenging for the most seasoned, the course features elevated tees, strategically bunkered greens and fairways, multi-tiered greens, several water hazards, and black sand traps.

The 18-hole championship course is framed by majestic pine trees and fir trees, and it features a memorable backdrop of the Monashee and Selkirk Mountains. Ideally located along the Kettle River, just minutes from its namesake lake, right between Spokane and Kelowna, the course is a destination all by itself.

The club often plays host to weddings, family gatherings, and corporate functions, not to mention an array of exciting tournaments throughout the year. Nearby accommodations cater to any comfort level—from posh lodges to cozy bed-and-breakfasts to quaint inns and RV parks. A British Columbia landmark since 1962, Christina Lake Golf Club is regularly ranked as one of the province's best.

Box 268, Christina Lake BC
250.447.9313 www.christinalakegolfclub.com

Photograph courtesy of Christina Lake Golf Club

DELTA GRAND OKANAGAN RESORT & ROYAL PRIVATE RESIDENCE CLUB

The Water Street address says it all—Delta Grand Okanagan & Royal Private Residence Club both sit proudly on the downtown Kelowna waterfront. Located in the heart of BC's wine country, Delta celebrates the fruits of the region by serving local food and wine in its restaurant, lounge, and banquet facility. Open since 1992, the resort is a steadfast part of the local community and landscape, and the committed staff take their role as stewards of the environment seriously.

Delta is endowed with authentically warm Canadian hospitality, perfect for introducing out-of-town guests to the magic and beauty of British Columbia and the Okanagan Valley.

Relax by the pool or on the beach; stroll downtown; tour the arts and cultural district; visit nearby wineries for tastings; or enjoy a day of golf, boating, or cycling. Whether traveling on business or leisure, you're at the centre of it all. From guest rooms and suites with jaw-dropping vistas to waterfront villas that provide all the comforts of home, the acclaimed resort showcases the best of the Okanagan.

1310 Water Street, Kelowna
250.763.4500 www.deltagrandokanagan.com

Photographs by Shawn Talbot and John Bilodeau

HAVANA ROOM @ MINIT MARKET

For Havana Room owner Jonathan Wright, a good cigar is not just a luxury, it's a passion—and a rich, heady passport to another enticing destination. Noticing a dearth in the marketplace among Kelowna's other premier offerings, including wine, golf, skiing, and dining, he was inspired to add top-shelf cigars to the mix. The store inside Minit Market boasts the largest selection of cigars in the region, along with humidors, lighters, pipes, tobacco, and smoker accessories.

Warm and inviting, the humidity-controlled, walk-in humidor is fully lined with Spanish cedar and houses not only Havana Room's specialty—Cuban cigars—but also a wide selection of the finest cigars from other top producers, including the Dominican Republic, Europe, Honduras, Indonesia, and Nicaragua. Beyond the impressive range of products available, what really sets the store apart is the group of in-house experts who possess extensive knowledge and can assist in helping guests travel the world of cigars to find the perfect match for their taste.

107-1835 Dilworth Drive, Kelowna
250.762.3737 www.havanaroom.ca

Photographs by Havana Room @ Minit Market

KELOWNA ACTORS STUDIO DINNER THEATRE

When was the last time you went to the theater? Chances are, it's been too long. Kelowna Actors Studio is looking to change that, one theatergoer at a time, by welcoming visitors to the only licensed dinner theater in Okanagan. Since opening in 2003, it's become a cultural stronghold in the community and seeks to bring in visitors from outside the region, showing off Kelowna's local flavor. The studio works at "providing quality education, entertainment and enrichment for all ages through the performing arts," according to its mission statement.

Founders Nate Flavel and Randy Leslie began the studio more than a decade ago, sharing their passion for drama and the arts. In addition to acting in, directing, and producing plays, the team has taught students of all ages, with some going on to Sheridan College in Toronto and the Julliard School in Manhattan. Both the students and the audience benefit tremendously, as renditions of Broadway's most beloved productions and musical dramas take the stage at the Kelowna Actors Studio.

1379 Ellis Street, Kelowna
250.862.2867 www.kelownaactorsstudio.com

Photographs by Glenna Turnbull

KETTLE VALLEY STEAM RAILWAY

In the heart of British Columbia's Okanagan Valley, a steam locomotive still rumbles along a small section of the famous Kettle Valley Railway, showcasing an integral piece of the province's railway history.

Completed in 1916, the 325-mile-long railway opened up the southern interior of BC to the rest of Canada and its minerals and fruit to world markets. But this line was no easy feat. Although the Canadian Pacific Railway had long been present in British Columbia, no tracks had made it into the southern part of the province because of the mountainous geography. But Kettle Valley Railway president J.J. Warren and Canadian Pacific Railway magnate Sir Thomas Shaughnessy collaborated to push the railway into existence. With service connecting the area from Midway in the Kootenays to Hope in the Fraser Canyon, the line snaked its way over and around three mountain ranges—and was said to be one of the most difficult railways ever built. Included in construction was the Trout Creek Bridge, a major feature—at 619 feet long and 238 feet high, it was the third largest steel girder bridge in North America at the time.

That legacy lives on today thanks to the Kettle Valley Steam Railway, a heritage railway attraction that sees more than 25,000 visitors each year. Powered by a restored 1912 steam locomotive, it traverses the only remaining section of the historic railway. The ride takes you through the rural beauty of Summerland and over the Trout Creek Bridge, offering 90 minutes of breathtaking views, live music, and historical commentary.

PO Box 1288, 18404 Bathville Road, Summerland
877.494.8424 www.kettlevalleyrail.org

Photograph by Doug Campbell

NARAMATA BENCH WINERIES ASSOCIATION

Fine wine delivers its own uniqueness in every bottle—a distinctive story that starts in the vineyard. The Naramata Bench Wineries Association is in the business of sharing the wines, experiences, and varied tales of its 25 renowned wineries, which are nestled along a meandering country road on the east side of Okanagan Lake in the heart of the southern Okanagan, one of Canada's premier grape-growing regions and a top destination for wine enthusiasts.

Picturesque Naramata Bench wine country is full of flavor and resonates with spectacular natural beauty. Wineries and vineyards are situated above sweeping clay cliffs that rise up from Okanagan Lake, dotting the rolling hills that upwardly climb to gentle mountains.

Not only defined by world-class wineries, the area has also become home to savory eateries, charming accommodations, and unique artisans, all enhancing this Okanagan getaway.

While each winery in the association has its own original wine specialties and philosophy of winemaking, what unites the group is a commitment to quality and authenticity amid friendly and relaxed surroundings. In that spirit, association members work together to create exceptional and fun wine events and experiences in all four seasons, with their famous Tailgate Party hosted every September.

www.naramatabench.com

Photographs by Tina Baird

OLIVER TWIST ESTATE WINERY

Everyone has a story, it seems, from back in the good old days, which makes a visit to Oliver Twist Estate Winery a trip down memory lane. The folks here just love to listen to these stories as they run their friendly tasting room, winery, and 17-acre vineyard.

Chances are you will see an old classic car on site and lots of nostalgic memorabilia inside the wine shop. In fact, they even created a new wine series called "NOSTALGIA" based on this theme featuring fancy hot rods with cute pin up girls on the labels. Rockabilly Red is sure to be one you won't want to miss.

The hands-on approach, along with the attention to detail, ensure that the highest quality vinifera grapes are grown in the vineyard. The attention to detail continues throughout the entire winemaking process. The winery offers a large selection of wines: from dry to off-dry whites and roses, medium to full-bodied reds, dessert, port, and late harvest, and is best known for its dry Kerner—a rarity in the region.

Guests can meet the forever entertaining staff and all of the team that plays a huge role in this young family-operated business. Customers may then relax with an impromptu picnic on one of the estate's scenic patios, taking in the valley views of the rugged desert hills, vineyards, and orchards.

398 Lupine Lane, Oliver
250.485.0227 www.olivertwistwinery.com

Photographs courtesy of Oliver Twist Estate Winery

RED ROOSTER WINERY

Red Rooster Winery released its first vintage in 1997. Soon after, the winery began producing award-winning wines that expressed the best of British Columbia and the Okanagan. Led by winemaker Karen Gillis, Red Rooster takes a gentle approach to winemaking that involves minimal intervention. While specific processes vary from varietal to varietal, all of its wines are fruit forward with the intent of bringing out the best features of the land. Karen believes quality winemaking requires a hands-on, roll-up-your-sleeves method, and her belief comes through in every bottle.

Karen and the staff at Red Rooster also believe in hospitality, which led to creating educational wine seminars held in The Coop, a private tasting boutique on the second floor.

The Pecking Room Patio Grill has a wonderful farm-to-table menu allowing you to sit and sip while overlooking the vineyard and Lake Okanagan. And the statue of the naked guy, well, he raises a few eyebrows. Drink up!

891 Naramata Road, Penticton
250.492.2424 www.redroosterwinery.com

Photographs: right and top left courtesy of Andrew Peller Limited; middle left by Jennifer Islaub; bottom right by Simon Henry

STACY STUDIOS

It's hard to find a corner of the art world that Marcia and Ron Stacy haven't explored. Practicing their craft since 1978, the couple has worked in both commercial and fine art with a variety of mediums: paint, sculpture, screen printing, and more. All of the works are equally impressive, capturing a variety of emotions and displaying a broad range of skill at Stacy Studios. Marcia's style offers a whimsical feel with works like her signature Celebration series; she evokes a sense of delight and joy for onlookers. Ron tends to focus on more serious topics like regional landscapes and still lifes. His metaphorical raven series has garnered attention, and he gives Northwest Coast mythology a face through sharp, telling images. Their talents perfectly balance one another.

Both artists understand the importance of community and stay connected in more ways than creating art. Marcia serves as director of the Community Arts Council, initiating the Summerland Studio Tour, bringing attention to the area's culture. The couple is always happy to show their artwork, although the studio gallery does not keep regular hours. Booking an appointment is the best way to see the collection.

14417 Biagioni Avenue, Summerland
250.486.8339 www.stacystudios.com

Photographs by Ron and Marcia Stacy

VAN WESTEN VINEYARDS

Great wine isn't made, it's grown. At Van Westen Vineyards, they have a similar philosophy. Simply put, the winery doesn't manufacture wine; instead the winemaking team led by Robert Van Westen creates great wine from the soil, up. The Van Westen family has been in the area for six decades and is the largest cherry growing family in Naramata. Robert counts himself lucky to be able to farm the land that was his grandfather's and father's before him. And the family has always been serious about the land. At Van Westen's winery, visitors will find basic buildings and a no-frills attitude. Robert is far more concerned with the tree fruit still harvested from the family's orchards and the wine grapes that go into the bottle.

Ranked the Eighth Best Winery in Canada by the judges at the 2012 Canadian Wine Access Awards, Van Westen Vineyards offers tastings in the production facility.

There, guests get a chance to speak one-on-one with the knowledgeable staff and can ask questions of Robert while sampling Van Westen's award-winning wines. Rather than charging tasting room fees, Van Westen Vineyards suggests donations, which go to BC Children's Hospital.

2800A Aikins Loop, Naramata
250.496.0067 www.vanwestenvineyards.com

Photographs by Preserved Light Photography

THE WELLNESS SPA

There are nice massages and there are life-changing massages. The Wellness Spa in Kelowna is well known for the latter, and not just among patrons. The owner, Sharon Strang, teaches courses on intuitive massage for professionals to develop their technical skills at a new level and for enthusiasts who want to learn about the art and even turn it into a career. Massage has physical benefits but also nurtures the sacred mind-body connection and promotes the flow of positive energy. Sharon is known as a healing bodyworker, and she has surrounded herself with a special group of similarly talented spa professionals who are focused on providing healthful, luxurious services to their discriminating clientele. They combine ancient knowledge about fostering inner beauty with modern methods to promote outer beauty. Whether you just need a few minutes of chair massage care or you're due for a two-hour-long hot stone massage makeover, they are delighted to help.

Along with myriad options for massage, The Wellness Spa's enticing array of services encompasses nine facials including a signature anti-aging facial, marine-based treatments, aesthetic services, foot reflexology, and full-body aroma wraps. These more traditional offerings are complemented by the powerful, nonphysical relaxation technique of Reiki. Soothing muscles, purifying skin, and nurturing spirit, The Wellness Spa takes a decidedly holistic approach to relaxation and rejuvenation.

Located within Best Western Plus Kelowna, an ecologically responsible hotel that uses geothermal power, The Wellness Spa is known for its earth-friendly practices and commitment to bettering the community. The spa's mantra of "well-balanced, well-being, well-deserved" reaches from its architectural confines to the many people who benefit from its healthful services.

2402 Highway 97 North, Kelowna
250.860.4985 www.wellnessspa.ca

Photographs by Sian James

South Thompson Inn & Conference Centre, page 128

Shuswap Tourism, page 135

Hell's Gate Airtram, page 146

Shuswap Tourism, page 135

Quaaout Lodge & Spa at Talking Rock Golf Resort, page 131

THOMPSON

Kamloops Airport Limited, page 129

Secwepemc Museum and Heritage Park, page 140

KAMLOOPS AIRPORT LIMITED

Sometimes an airport isn't just an airport. Going beyond functionality, Kamloops Airport Limited serves as a cultural center and welcoming point for all travelers who come to British Columbia. It promotes and enhances the region by displaying local art throughout the airport grounds and maintaining close partnerships with nearby groups like the Thompson Okanagan Tourism Organization, Revelstoke Mountain Resort, and Kamloops Chamber of Commerce. With strategic planning and thoughtful conception, the airport has become an integral part of the city and its surrounding area.

The state-of-the-art facilities include two runways with an Instrument Landing System and a 1,500-square-metre terminal equipped with convenient check-in counters. Additionally the airport is home to industrial aviation operations, which includes a flight school, mechanical repair and rebuilding for small engines, aircraft salvage, a forest fire control centre, and avionics specialists. It has become its own economic force, providing jobs and creating growth for the community. Most recently, and impressively, there has been an 80 percent increase in travelers—thanks to the ingenuity and mission of the management team at Kamloops Airport Limited.

101 - 3035 Airport Road, Kamloops
250.376.3613 www.kamloopsairport.com

Photographs by Kent Wong

QUAAOUT LODGE & SPA AT TALKING ROCK GOLF RESORT

When the Little Shuswap Indian Band, led by Chief Oliver Arnouse, decided to open their land to the public, they made accessible a rich patchwork of culture, adventure, and history, all of which is captured at the Quaaout Lodge & Spa at Talking Rock Golf Resort. The charming and peaceful destination, located midway between Vancouver and Calgary, truly reflects its Shuswap name, Quaaout, which means "where the sun's rays hit the ground."

Tucked into a sublimely rural setting along the north shore of the unspoiled Little Shuswap Lake, the lodge features first-class accommodations, along with well-appointed conference facilities. Seventy serene guest rooms and suites, each with a personal balcony, overlook the tranquil water and a surrounding sea of tall pine trees and woods, providing the perfect respite after a day of exploration. Cultural coordinators at the lodge assist with area activities that range from canoeing to fishing, zip-lining, boating, and beyond. The property's rugged Talking Rock Golf Course, designed by esteemed Canadian architects Graham Cooke and Wayne Carlton, features 18 holes that traverse the diverse landscape, meandering through the natural forest setting and ending along Little Shuswap Lake.

Steeped in the colorful culture of the area, Quaaout also offers educational workshops and arts activities—from lessons about the medicine wheel and the way of the warrior to hands-on sessions for rock painting, beadwork, Birch bark basket-weaving, hand drum constructions, and moccasin making. The lodge's Jack Sam's Restaurant likewise honors the aboriginal, First Nation traditions of the region with its seasonal, locally sourced menu.

Photographs courtesy of Quaaout Lodge

Another major highlight is the promotion of healing and well-being at the property's Le7ke Spa, where a holistic wellness approach fuels relaxation and rejuvenation with conventional offerings as well as treatments derived from traditional native practices. Offering the ultimate in hospitality and enveloped in the natural beauty of its locale, Quaaout Lodge & Spa is a radiant, spiritual escape for visitors and local residents alike.

1663 Little Shuswap Lake Road, Chase
250.679.3090 www.quaaoutlodge.com

Photographs: above courtesy of Quaaout Lodge; left and facing page bottom by Darren Robinson

SHUSWAP TOURISM

If the enticing spirit of the Shuswap could be bottled, it would most certainly be an inviting tonic of beauty and intrigue tempered by a relaxed, down-to-earth attitude. The premier Canadian destination, which is centered around the renowned Shuswap Lake just north of the Okanagan region, is comprised of seven primary areas: Chase, South Shuswap, North Shuswap, Salmon Arm, Sicamous and Eagle Valley, Falkland, and Enderby—each delivering its own signature set of attractions and an impressive selection of activities.

Indeed, variety is truly the spice that seasons the Shuswap. With mild seasonal weather and captivating natural landscapes, including the compelling personality of the ever-present Shuswap Lake, along with alpine meadows, rolling trails and hills, wilderness, and forests, the region acts like a choose-your-own-adventure novel with boundless options to put on your must-do, can't-miss list. It's a place where you can plunge into the warm water from the deck of a houseboat an hour after playing the 18th hole. Or you can discover the hidden natural treasures of Margaret Falls, mountain bike and hike through Larch Hills traverse, or ski and snowshoe through the scenery, all before changing shoes for local wine-tasting, dining and savoring the views via resort-style relaxation, or park-side camping under the stars.

Photographs by Darren Robinson Photography

A quintessential Canadian cultural experience, the Shuswap also boasts a colorful array of museums, art galleries, events, and fests, such as the famous Roots and Blues Festival, that reflect its value on community not to mention the storied history of the Shuswap First Nations—the Secwepemc—an important Salish nation of tribal bands whose ancestors have always lived in the British Columbia interior. Shuswap Tourism features six visitor centers in the area, where vacationers can easily kick-start exploration, create personalized itineraries, and soak in all the possibilities of a Shuswap getaway.

781 Marine Park Drive NE, Salmon Arm
250.833.5928 www.shuswaptourism.com

Photographs: above, top left, and facing page Darren Robinson Photography; top right by Kari Medig

SOUTH THOMPSON INN & CONFERENCE CENTRE

Capturing all the elegance of a traditional Kentucky-style ranch, South Thompson Inn & Conference Centre sits just 15 minutes east of Kamloops on land that was once home to thoroughbred racing stables. The original brick manor house and stables remain, with 55 sprawling acres of the region's most beautiful terrain as the backdrop. Accommodations include a variety of 57 individually appointed guest rooms, all with balconies overlooking the river or mountains—a far cry from the standard hotel setting.

Even pets are welcome here, since they're considered family members for so many visitors. Relaxed and secluded, South Thompson Inn & Conference Centre offers upscale, casual sophistication and gives visitors a chance to unwind, taking in everything the countryside has to offer. The inn has received wide recognition and multiple hospitality honors, as well as attracting the likes of Bill Gates and the Prime Minister of Singapore.

Owner David Patriquin has carefully preserved all of the charm from the original design and added genuine hospitality with a management team that will go out of their way to give guests an unforgettable visit. The staff will even help coordinate activities: candlelight dinners on the riverfront gazebo, hikes through scenic trails, or an old-fashioned campfire with sing-a-longs and s'mores. Every trip is as distinctly personal as it is memorable.

3438 Shuswap Road East, Kamloops
250.573.3777 www.stigr.com

Photographs: top by Branden Deschenes; above and facing page courtesy of South Thompson Inn & Conference Centre

SECWEPEMC MUSEUM AND HERITAGE PARK

At the heart of the Secwepemc Museum and its Heritage Park is an unswerving passion and purpose to preserve and perpetuate the entire spectrum of Secwepemc culture, both past and present, breathing life into the vibrant story of the people indigenous to the land. Guided tours through time; legends and stories told round a crackling fire in an underground pit house; powwow grounds for traditional dances, drumming, food, and games; and the sights and sounds of wildlife in the surrounding marsh—it's all part of the unique educational destination, which is also the first Indian-owned museum in the interior of British Columbia.

Located on the Kamloops Indian Band, the museum is the former site of the Kamloops Indian Residential School, one of the few school buildings still in existence. Indoor exhibits are filled with historical and contemporary photographs, illustrations, and artifacts, while innovative workshops and classes further promote the native traditions and language.

Outdoor cultural displays permeate Heritage Park, where the 2,000-year-old archaeological remains of a village site include four reconstructed winter homes, summer tule mat lodges, and various food preparation structures, where scheduled performances bring the setting to life. Ethno-botanical gardens house five different ecological zones with many plants still used by the Secwepemc for food, medicine, and tools.

With such a colorful and diverse range of offerings, the mission of the Secwepemc to share their living and thriving culture is palpable—as is their fervent desire to honor and sustain their heritage.

200-330 Chief Alex Thomas Way, Kamloops
250.828.9749 www.secwepemcmuseum.com

Photographs by Nacoma George

TWIN ANCHORS HOUSEBOATS

Although vacationing on a floating resort may sound like something out of a dream, there is a freshwater location just between Shuswap and Mara Lakes where this is very much a reality. Twin Anchors Marina is home to Twin Anchors Houseboats, a groundbreaking, family owned company that has become Canada's largest houseboat vacation company since its 1964 inception. Twin Anchors is renowned for its legendary hospitality and luxurious houseboats, and Shuswap Lake provides the ultimate backdrop for an unforgettable nautical adventure with more than 1,000 kilometres of shoreline for guests to discover. The Sicamous location offers guests a licensed restaurant overlooking the Sicamous Channel, plenty of parking, and a gift shack. Guests may also choose to depart from the Salmon Arm marina—also on Shuswap Lake.

The houseboats range from the intimate Cruiser, which is perfect for a small family or couple looking for a lake getaway, to the fully loaded CruiseCraft V that accommodates up to 24 people. This premium model includes three full bathrooms—one with a steam shower—10 staterooms, custom hot tub, two slides, and an impressive entertainment area. Built exclusively at Twin Anchors Marine Manufacturing, the houseboats are custom made and designed to give guests the best possible experience while houseboating in British Columbia.

101 Martin Street, Sicamous
250.836.2450 www.twinanchors.com

Photographs by Don Weixl / Twin Anchors Houseboats

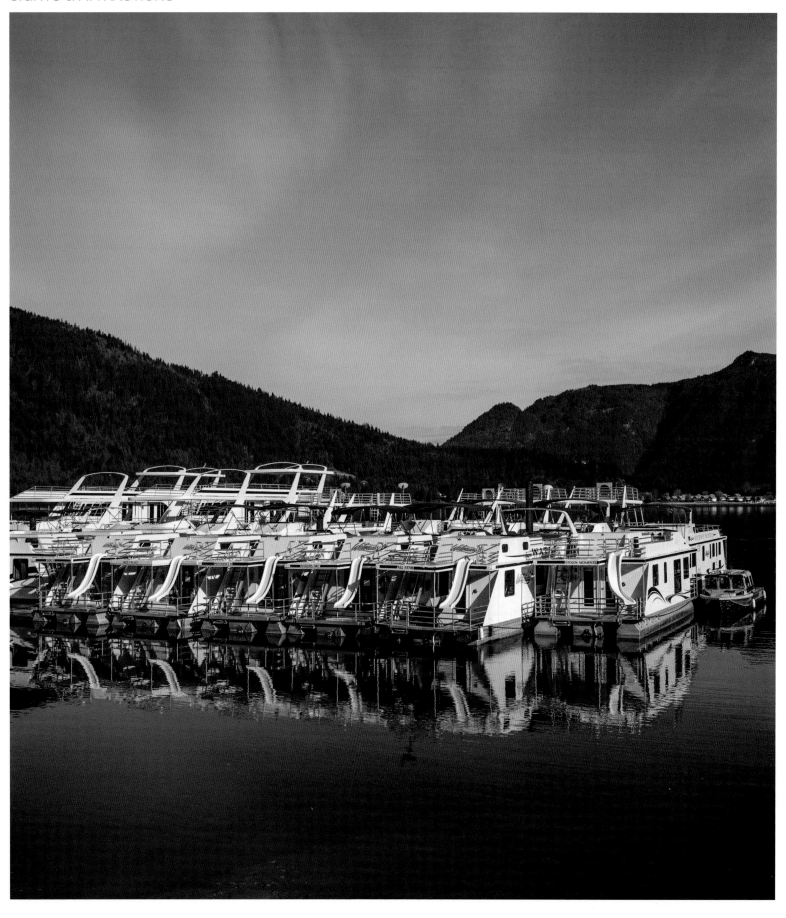

WATERWAY HOUSEBOATS

The only thing better than being lakefront is being on the beautiful Shuswap Lake itself, staying in the world-class Waterway Houseboats. The magnificent lake, halfway between Calgary and Vancouver, is a year-round recreation and houseboating paradise.

Nestled among the vast British Columbia mountain valleys, sun drenched beaches, beautiful waterfalls, and awesome fishing are ready for discovery from the comfort of your home away from home.

Imagine watching sunsets, relaxing in the onboard hot tub, or splashing down the waterslide of your own floating private resort. Or for a more active vacation, enjoy swimming, hiking, water-skiing, golfing, ATV riding, and mountain biking.

The company has an impressive fleet of 60 luxurious houseboats that comfortably accommodate groups from 10 to 30. Every boat goes though an intensive 200-point inspection, ensuring that guests will have a truly first-class houseboat vacation.

Waterway Houseboats doesn't just offer a place to stay; it provides unique accommodations with a splash of adventure.

1 Mervyn Road, Sicamous
877.928.3792 www.waterwayhouseboats.com

Photographs by Miller Photographics

HELL'S GATE AIRTRAM

Although explorer Simon Fraser reported that he had "encountered the gates of hell" when he scaled the canyon walls along the Fraser River in 1808, it simply feels like an exciting, fun adventure to take in that same scenery while safely aboard a Hell's Gate Airtram. This locally owned and operated attraction sponsors many local organizations, such as the Fraser Canyon Hospice Society, and hosts seasonal events that are immensely enjoyable for locals and visitors alike.

The excursion departs from highway level on a spacious tram that descends over Hell's Gate—the narrowest part of the Fraser River at only 33 meters wide, boasting twice the volume of Niagara Falls' water—and the International Fishways, which assist the millions of salmon each year that journey home to their spawning grounds. Before the trams ascend back to highway level, a stop at the lower terminal offers a suspension bridge, education center, café with mouthwatering salmon chowder, a decadent fudge and ice cream shop, and gold panning activities to engage each visitor.

43111 Trans-Canada Highway, Boston Bar
604.867.9277 www.hellsgateairtram.com

Photographs courtesy of Hell's Gate Airtram

NORTH THOMPSON FALL FAIR & RODEO ASSOCIATION

What began as a small fair for 4-H youngsters and local farmers in 1950 has grown to one of the leading events in the Thompson Nicola Regional District, with as many as 11,000 annual visitors. The North Thompson Fall Fair & Rodeo Association was first run by manager Len Johnson, who worked closely with local families to create entertainment while promoting the farm and ranch lifestyle. As Len once stated, the fair is "a celebration of agriculture, livestock, western country living, and community spirit," and it has remained so to this day. The North Thompson Fall Fair & Rodeo Association relies heavily on its hard working volunteers who make the event a resounding success each year on Labour Day weekend. The three-day event features family focused activities: parades, pancake breakfasts, heavy horse pulls, tractor races, pony chuckwagon races, 4-H, BCRA Rodeo, and more.

The impressive 36,000-square-foot North Thompson Agriplex has also been filled with the sights and sounds of the annual fair since 2011. The facilities include a spacious indoor arena, animal pens, offices, and a banquet hall. Additionally, there is an outdoor rodeo arena with grandstand-style seating, two banquet halls, picnic space, camping space, and barns to house an array of farm animals.

PO Box 873, Barriere
250.319.8023 www.fallfair-rodeo.com

Photographs: left and bottom right by Jill Hayward; top right courtesy of North Thompson Star/Journal

INDEX

Penticton, British Columbia, page 77

Sandhill Winery, page 94

THE PANACHE COLLECTION

Dream Homes Series

An Exclusive Showcase of the Finest Architects, Designers and Builders

Carolinas, Chicago, Coastal California, Colorado, Deserts, Florida, Georgia, Los Angeles, Metro New York, Michigan, Minnesota, New England, New Jersey, Northern California, Ohio & Pennsylvania, Pacific Northwest, Philadelphia, South Florida, Southwest, Tennessee, Texas, Washington, D.C., Extraordinary Homes California

Spectacular Homes Series

An Exclusive Showcase of the Finest Interior Designers

California, Carolinas, Chicago, Colorado, Florida, Georgia, Heartland, London, Michigan, Minnesota, New England, Metro New York, Ohio & Pennsylvania, Pacific Northwest, Philadelphia, South Florida, Southwest, Tennessee, Texas, Toronto, Washington, D.C., Western Canada

Perspectives on Design Series

Design Philosophies Expressed by Leading Professionals

California, Carolinas, Chicago, Colorado, Florida, Georgia, Great Lakes, London, Minnesota, New England, New York, Pacific Northwest, South Florida, Southwest, Toronto, Western Canada

Art of Celebration Series

Inspiration and Ideas from Top Event Professionals

Chicago & the Greater Midwest, Colorado, Georgia, New England, New York, Northern California, South Florida, Southern California, Southern Style, Southwest, Toronto, Washington, D.C.

City by Design Series

An Architectural Perspective

Atlanta, Charlotte, Chicago, Dallas, Denver, New York, Orlando, Phoenix, San Francisco, Texas

Spectacular Wineries Series

A Captivating Tour of Established, Estate and Boutique Wineries

California's Central Coast, Napa Valley, New York, Ontario, Oregon, Sonoma County, Texas, Washington

Experience Series

The Most Interesting Attractions, Hotels, Restaurants, and Shops

Austin & the Hill Country, British Columbia, Thompson Okanagan

Interiors Series

Leading Designers Reveal Their Most Brilliant Spaces

Florida, Midwest, New York, Southeast, Washington, D.C.

Golf Series

The Most Scenic and Challenging Golf Holes

Deserts, Colorado, Ontario, Pacific Northwest, Southeast, Texas, Western Canada

Weddings Series

Captivating Destinations and Exceptional Resources Introduced by the Finest Event Planners

Southern California

Specialty Titles

Publications about Architecture, Interior Design, Wine, and Hospitality

21st Century Homes, Distinguished Inns of North America, Into the Earth: A Wine Cave Renaissance, Luxurious Interiors, Napa Valley Iconic Wineries, Shades of Green Tennessee, Signature Homes, Spectacular Hotels, Spectacular Restaurants of Texas, Visions of Design

Custom Titles

Publications by Renowned Experts and Celebrated Institutions

Cloth and Culture: Couture Creations of Ruth E. Funk, Colonial: The Tournament, Dolls Etcetera, Geoffrey Bradfield Ex Arte, Lake Highland Preparatory School: Celebrating 40 Years, Family Is All That Matters

Panache Books App

Inspiration at Your Fingertips

Download the Panache Books app in the iTunes Store to access select Panache Partners publications. Each book offers inspiration at your fingertips.